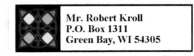

Preparing
to Serve
at the Table

John G. Hibbard

NOVALIS

THE LITURGICAL PRESS

Design: Eye-to-Eye Design, Toronto

Layout: Suzanne Latourelle

Illustrations: Eugene Kral

Series Editor: Bernadette Gasslein

© 1997, Novalis, Saint Paul University, Ottawa, Ontario, Canada

Business Office: Novalis, 49 Front Street East, 2nd floor, Toronto, Ontario M5E 1B3

Novalis: ISBN 2 89088 808 8

The Liturgical Press: ISBN 0-8146-2507-x
A Liturgical Press Book
Published in the United States of America by The Liturgical Press, Box 7500, Collegeville, MN 56321-7500
Library of Congress data available on request.

Printed in Canada.

Hibbard, John G. (John Gordon), 1948
    Preparing to serve at the table

(Preparing for liturgy)

Includes bibliographical references.

ISBN 2-89088-808-8

1. Lord's Supper–Lay celebration–Catholic Church. 2. Catholic Church–Liturgy. I. Title. II. Series.

BV195.5.H52 1997   264L02036   C97-900971-5

Contents

Introduction

Welcome to the world of ministry and service. I use the word "world" because serving will introduce you to many new words, places, things and concepts. Once you begin to serve, people may use many strange words that you've never heard before (see the glossary for a list of these words). They will talk of the tabernacle, explain how to hold the sacramentary, and indicate when to place the corporal and purificator on the altar. You will carry candles to the ambo and carry the thurible in the entrance procession. Sound frightening? Don't worry. This book is for you, to introduce you to this new world of church words and language.

What Is a Server?

First, let's talk about what a server is. The server is a minister, a person who serves the parish community. As a minister, the server assists the community to celebrate the sacred liturgy, that is to worship God, especially at the Sunday eucharist. While you will mainly assist the priest to lead the people of God in prayer, you also help all the people in church to pray and worship God. Through the sharing of your talents and by the graceful and reverent way that you perform your tasks, you will contribute to the spirit of prayer and worship. While knowing what to do is important, more is needed. You must know something about liturgy: what it is, how it unfolds, why it is done as it is and when it happens.

Serving is more than helping others. It is about who and what we are. It is a living out of our baptism as the people of God and those united to Jesus Christ. Today in our world Jesus continues his work through his body, the church, which is all Christian people. Serving in the parish is a way of living the new life of Jesus and of being Jesus for others around us. Naturally, being a baptized Christian is more that what we do in church: it is the way we live at home, school, and play; it is how we treat and live with others. Serving in our parish church reflects what we do all the time.

To those who are responsible for the training of servers in the parish, I offer this word of advice. Do not think only of young people when you think of those who serve at the altar. Encouraging young people to exercise this liturgical ministry is important, but do not segregate youth in one or two ministries: integrate them into the parish, encouraging them to minister as their talents indicate. Encourage talented adults to serve as well. Recruiting young people as servers only to involve them somehow in the church or having servers only because it gives young people something to do does not do justice to young people or to the gifts they possess. Rather, it indicates a lack of understanding that ministry springs forth from baptism. Furthermore, it does not relate ministry to the whole assembly, or take seriously the ministry of serving itself. As in the case of other ministries, talent, ability and desire must be important components for serving the liturgical assembly. All ministries should attempt to reflect a broad cross-section of a parish, involving youth and adults, men and women. This book does not presume that serving is for children or young people only, but for those who demonstrate the necessary talent to assist the assembly in the prayerful and reverent unfolding of the liturgy of the church.

I am thankful that, in the parish in which I grew up, serving was a serious ministry. Most servers were in high school; a few were in university. Those responsible for our training treated us as valuable members of the Christian community. We were proud of our contributions, and, in the days when liturgy was changing from Latin to English, it was not unheard of for the priests of the parish to consult the older servers on how to best implement the changes of Vatican II. I hope that this confidence and respect will develop in all servers, and especially in those who assist, encourage and support them.

This book must, by its nature, remain general. The size and layout of your church building, the contours of your worship space, the available resources and the options of the liturgy dictate a healthy diversity. The majority of the material presented in this book emphasizes a knowledge of basic liturgical principles as well as a "how to do it" approach. Obviously, both are important, but the limits of space impose restrictions on the amount of material that can be presented. This book is presented as a beginning only.

General Liturgical Principles

Serving is a true liturgical ministry. In the big picture, it is a service to the gathering of God's people called the assembly, and it takes place during the worship of this assembly. Many see the server only as an assistant to the priest. In some ways this is true, for the server holds the book of prayers (sacramentary), holds the wine and water as they are placed in the cup or chalice and washes the hands of the priest. However, a more detailed examination shows that servers assist the liturgy by leading all the ministers in procession into and out of the worship area, by indicating to the assembly the important signs of the liturgy by carrying candles in front of the cross, the Lectionary, and the book of the gospels, by assisting the deacon, and by making sure that what is needed for the celebration is brought, carried or moved into place. The server truly assists the priest, and the other ministers the whole people assembled.

Probably more than any other ministry, servers are concerned with detail and with almost every aspect of the celebration of the liturgy. While lectors must be familiar with the Lectionary and the ambo, and communion ministers with the altar and sacred vessels, servers must know all of these things and more. It is an important and difficult ministry to master. For this reason I wonder if it is fair to entrust this ministry only to children. For when children alone serve, there is a tendency to treat serving, not as a true ministry, but as a decoration. I have often been in churches where the servers carry the candles in and out of the celebration, but do little else.

Part of this problem may be due to the fact that serving was one of the few ministries of the laity that existed before the reforms of Vatican II. Then only young boys could serve. Perhaps with the restoration of the ministry of readers, cantors, deacons, hospitality, communion, etc., we have not had time to renew our vision of what serving is and its importance to the community. Either it has been abandoned or neglected as a ministry, or it has continued as it was from the beginning. When servers do little, it is probably because they have not received adequate training and preparation. This book will also help you develop a program of training for servers.

Step 1: Understanding the Liturgy

The first step to serving is to look at the larger picture of the church's worship, for we must talk about liturgy and the essential role that God's people exercise in it before looking at what the servers do.

Liturgy is the action of the body of Christ

Liturgy comes from a Greek word that means "public work." Our work is to worship God. By baptism each person is united to Jesus Christ. We are all children of God and brothers and sisters of Jesus. This large family, Saint Paul called the body of Christ. Like a body there are many different parts: fingers, hands, toes, legs, mouth, ears, nose, and so on. Each of us, as part of the body of Christ, is different, and has different abilities; above all we are one in Jesus. Therefore, in the liturgy, whatever we do, we do in union with Christ; what Christ does, we do with him. Liturgy is the action of the body of Christ. It is the action of Jesus Christ, the high priest, who carries on his ministry in the midst of people of every age and time, and it is the action of the whole people of God. Thus, liturgy is both the action of Jesus and the church.

Liturgy is praise and intercession

The work of liturgy or worship is to praise God and continue the mission of Jesus in this world. We do this all through life and in the church when we gather to praise God and pray for the ongoing work of the salvation of all people. As the body of Christ, we recall God's action among us and give praise and thanks for what God does through Jesus Christ, and by the power of the Holy Spirit. As a server your work is also to praise and thank God in the prayers, actions and songs of the liturgy.

Liturgy is a communal, ritual act

Liturgy is group work. In working together, we not only show that we are one with Jesus; we are also a sign to the world of God's presence and action among us. In liturgy, the people of God come together to witness to the world of God's love and action. Liturgy also makes us aware of God's presence among us, how God works today to build up the church and draws all people to salvation.

Liturgy uses symbol and ritual. The altar and cross, the Lectionary and the candles, bread and wine, the people themselves are the symbols used in liturgy. Standing and sitting, bowing and singing, listening and responding are our ritual actions during the liturgy. In other words, liturgy speaks to us and draws us closer to God and one another through its own language and way of doing things.

Liturgy works best when we know what we're doing. Therefore, liturgy must change very little. When we do the same thing over and over again, we can learn our part. We call this a ritual. Ritual is part of life, just as the way our family may celebrate Christmas or Thanksgiving. We know what to expect, and how we fit in—and we look forward to it! Moreover, we're disappointed when someone forgets to do something.

Liturgy is a dialogue

Liturgy is like a conversation with God. God talks to us, and we respond. Liturgy is a dialogue between God and the assembly, between word and action, between the assembly and the priest. God calls all people to worship, and God's people respond by gathering on the Lord's Day to worship. Therefore, we read God's word at the liturgy.

When the word of God is proclaimed in the liturgy, Christ himself speaks to the church, and the word calls to mind what God has done, so that we may join our voices in praise and thanksgiving. When we hear what God has done in the past, we remember that God is still with us and wants to do wonderful works for us as well.

Liturgy is the celebration of the paschal mystery

If liturgy is work, it is joyful work, that is, a celebration. We celebrate Jesus, his life, his death and resurrection, his sending of the Holy Spirit, and everything he has done for us. We gather to celebrate our new life that we receive from him. This is called the paschal (or Easter) mystery. The most important act of our salvation is that God sent Jesus into human history to save the world. In recalling what God has done, we don't just remember the past, but, by remembering, bring God's saving action into our lives now. If God saved the people of the past, God is still acting in the world to save us.

Liturgy is a mystery, not because we cannot understand what is happening (God is working in our midst and in our lives), but because, in the wondrous union of Jesus with us, God works among us. The word "mystery" was the ancient Greek word we now translate as "sacrament." Through visible signs the unseen God continues the work of our salvation. The paschal mystery is not just about Jesus, for we are one with him through baptism. The paschal mystery is also about our life in Jesus Christ. It is about our suffering and service, and how God helps us to witness to Jesus and live as his disciples.

Liturgy centres around Sunday and the eucharist

The life and worship of the Christian community centres around Sunday and the celebration of the eucharist. Sunday is the first day of the week, the day God began creating the universe. It is the day God raised Jesus from the dead and sent the Holy Spirit on the church. On the first day of the week, Jesus appeared to the disciples after his resurrection, broke bread and ate with them. Faithful to what Jesus did, we, his disciples, gather together on this day to celebrate Jesus' death and resurrection and the sending of the Holy Spirit. Faithful to what he did, we celebrate the eucharist, our primary way of entering into his paschal mystery.

Liturgy expresses the church's faith

We gather together on Sunday because we believe in God, in Jesus Christ, in the Holy Spirit, and in the holy catholic church, and we want others to know it. We believe that God loves us and still acts among us. We believe that as his co-workers we are to carry out Jesus' mission. Even coming to church tells people that we believe; this is our faith in action. God's word is being translated into action. Although faith is an intensely personal thing, it is not something that is exclusively ours. Faith is God's gift that we receive through a community: from parents, teachers and other Christians. We share our faith *with* others, because we have received this faith *from* others. Moreover, to grow and remain healthy, faith needs to be nurtured and affirmed in a community of believers. This happens in the liturgy. Liturgy expresses, shapes and affirms the belief of the church, and allows the members of the assembly to implement in their lives what they celebrate together.

Step 2: Understanding Liturgical Ministry

Worship is more than reciting prayers, listening to words or doing holy things. It is an action of a group of people who believe that God sent Jesus to bring salvation, and the Holy Spirit to make us a holy and priestly people. To make this activity happen, the community of God's people needs assistance.

Ordained leadership is one ministry. Other ministers help the assembly to carry out its sacred action. They include not only people who assist during the liturgy, but, in a broader sense, those who prepare the liturgy, the place of worship and the things that we need for worship. Servers are among these ministers.

The ministry of servers

Servers at the eucharist or any other liturgical celebration assist the whole community, the body of Christ. They usually help the person, the priest or presider, who leads the community's worship. While this might be a priest (an ordained presbyter or bishop), it may also include a lay person who leads the prayer of a community in the absence of a priest. As a server, you help the leader to exercise the ministry of presiding. You also help to direct the attention of the community to the use of symbols during the celebration.

To truly be a server means to be a servant—to help others. To be a true servant, remember that you are present to help.

The ministry of training servers

Recognizing that the main users of this book may not be servers themselves, but those who help prepare and train others for this ministry, I offer a few comments.

- If you were or are a server, try to remember your own experience and training. What helped you? What did you find difficult?

- Don't try to teach everything at once. Schedule several training sessions. Most of us learn by seeing and doing. The role of repetition is invaluable. Don't be afraid to repeat.

- Consistency in how servers serve is important. This is important especially if there are several priests who preside at the liturgy. It also applies to the instructions that those who prepare the servers give to them.

- Explaining the "why" is as important as the "how." Ministers are not robots, but living individuals who belong to the worshipping community. It helps to know why actions are done in a particular manner. In other words, seeing the larger picture helps servers see their contribution and how it fits into the whole liturgy.

- Use everyday examples to explain what happens in church on Sunday and what servers do. If you are not good at doing this, consult someone who is. For example, draw a parallel to receiving a visitor at home and at the celebration of the eucharist. We welcome visitors to our home at the door and lead them into the living room for a time of conversation. Only after this dialogue and exchange of ideas and friendship do we move to the table.

  We prepare the table with a cloth and candles, setting it with the necessary utensils, cups and plates, and bring the food to the table and serve it. When all is prepared, we are ready to eat and drink. Giving thanks for food and friendship is a usual part of the meal before we eat and drink. Closing rites and farewells bring the meal and the visit to a close.

  So it is in the eucharist. The procession from the entrance to the worship area, our listening and responding to God's word, setting the table, bringing the bread and wine, saying the prayer of thanksgiving, serving, eating and drinking are part of what the eucharist is all about.

- Grouping tasks together may help the servers remember what they have to do. For example, group the number of times an action or object is used: the candles are carried three times, there are three tasks to preparing the altar, there are three tasks to be done after communion, the sacramentary is held three times.

- Invite the servers to look for or be attentive to cues: as soon as the gospel acclamation begins, get the candles; as soon as the collection starts, place the sacramentary and cup on the altar; as soon as the sign of peace finishes, bring the extra plates and cups to the altar for communion, etc.

Step 3: Understanding the Eucharist

The eucharist consists of two parts: the liturgy of the word and the liturgy of the eucharist. Each part has a rite of preparation: the introductory rites prepare for the liturgy of the word, and the preparation of the altar and gifts prepares for the liturgy of the eucharist. The liturgy of the word takes place at the ambo (lectern) and consists of readings from sacred scripture and the response of the community in silence, word, gesture and song. The liturgy of the eucharist takes place at the altar and consists of taking bread and cup to the altar; praying the great prayer of thanksgiving over the bread and cup; breaking bread (and pouring the consecrated wine into several cups); and giving communion.

The liturgy of the word

In the proclamation of the word the whole people of God actively listen to God's word and respond to it in silence and song. Jesus speaks to the assembly, inviting us to share the good news of the paschal mystery. The assembly responds joyfully to this good news in silence, song and awe.

The liturgy of the word includes many elements: the proclamation of the scriptures, followed by a time of silence to respond to and reflect on God's word; singing the psalm and acclamation as a response to the word and an expression of our joy; a procession of the gospel book to greet and rejoice at the presence of Jesus; a homily, based on the word; a profession/response of faith in the creed; intercession for the building up of the church and the salvation of the world.

Servers are involved in the actions which surround the liturgy of the word. They carry the candles and incense to accompany the Lectionary or the book of the gospels; with the people, they make the sign of the cross on their forehead, lips and heart at the gospel. As members of the assembly, they sit to listen to the first and second readings and the homily, stand to listen to the gospel, profess faith in the creed and make intercession. Music plays an important part in the liturgy of the word as it expresses the assembly's love and joy in response to God's word and acclaims the presence of Christ who speaks words of life and healing.

Liturgy of the eucharist

The liturgy of the eucharist consists of the Lord's four actions at the last supper. These centre around the bread and cup: taking, blessing, breaking and giving; they provide the structure and action of the liturgy of the eucharist: the preparation of the gifts, the eucharistic prayer, the fraction rite and the communion rite. In a different way each part is an action of the assembly.

During the preparation of the gifts, servers prepare the table as the collection begins. They place the corporal, the sacramentary, the chalice and the purificator on the altar. The presider may need them to help receive the gifts by placing the collection in an appropriate place and bringing the containers of wine and water to the altar. After the presider or deacon has placed the wine and water in the cup, servers return the pitchers or cruets to the side table. (When enough wine is needed for the communion of all the people, the container of wine remains on the altar.) Then they return to the altar to wash the hands of the priest.

During the preparation for communion they bring additional plates and cups for the bread and wine to the altar from the side table after the sign of peace. During or after communion, they help clear the altar, returning the sacramentary, corporal and other cloths and vessels to the side table. After a time of silence, they hold the sacramentary for the prayer after communion. Then, after the blessing, they lead the ministers to the main doors of the church.

In Summary

1. Liturgy is the action of all the people of God. When servers exercise their liturgical ministry, they are helping the assembly to express its faith in word, song and gesture, to dialogue with God in silence and song, and to praise God in word, song and deed.

2. Liturgy is the celebration of the paschal mystery of Jesus and centres around Sunday, the gathering of Jesus' disciples and the celebration of the eucharist.

3. The celebration of the eucharist consists of two main parts, the liturgy of the word and the liturgy of the eucharist. In the liturgy of the word, the gospel is the most important element; in the liturgy of the eucharist, the eucharistic prayer is the central element.

4. To be a good minister adequate knowledge, training and practice are necessary. These include recognizing the focal points of the liturgy of the word and the eucharist, and what is needed for the celebration of each.

Discussion Questions

1. What are some of the images or things that come to mind when you think of serving?

2. Discuss some of the common elements shared by the eucharist and a family meal.

3. In the celebration of the eucharist, how are the gospel and eucharistic prayer shown to be the two most important elements? What actions, acclamations, postures surround these two central elements? What is the role of the servers during each?

4. What are the actions of the people in the celebration of the eucharist?

General Principles of Serving

Serving is an act of faith and worship. Servers offer themselves, as Jesus did, for the benefit of others, the worshipping community. Servers must be willing to share their faith, time and talents with their parish community—to live out their baptismal anointing to be like Jesus. This is something for them to be nervous about, for this service to the parish community means a willingness both to learn more about ministry and to commit to the responsibility they are undertaking. A little nervousness may help them take their ministry seriously.

In exercising this ministry, servers will need prayerfulness and grace to add to the atmosphere of worship. This will affect everything they do, whether carrying a candle or bringing the chalice and sacramentary to the altar.

Step 1: Learning the Basics

Entering the world of the church building opens up a new world of sacred places, things and names. While objects may be familiar, they carry strange and unusual names. Learning a new language is part of the server's ministry. Some of these terms are found in the glossary.

Serving involves movement: carrying things, preparing things and doing things in public. Since liturgy is repeated action, training and doing the same thing over and over will help servers become comfortable. Don't get discouraged if it takes some time to learn everything or if training seems long. Practising such simple things as walking in procession, bowing or holding a book may seem unimportant at the time, but when servers have to do them in public for the first time, they will be glad for all the practice.

Coordination

Servers need some physical agility, discipline and coordination, so they don't trip or look awkward when walking, going up stairs, or genuflecting. They must also be able to act in conjunction with others, especially when walking with that person or presenting the wine and water to the priest. Learning to lead in a procession, walking behind another person or turning towards another rather than away from them are small but significant elements of coordination.

A. Processions

The basic movement in the liturgy is a procession. Processions are practical; they allow a group of people to move from one place to another, but processions have a greater significance:

- They make visible the faith of God's people who have gathered to celebrate.

- They call the community together in a corporate and communal act.

- They highlight who we are as God's holy people who walk in pilgrimage to the kingdom of God.

- They add an element of festivity and solemnity to the celebration.

The Sunday eucharist has at least five processions. The same people may not be involved in all the processions, and servers may not participate in all of them, but, whether they include a few people or many, processions are meant to affect the whole assembly of God's people.

Entrance procession

The entrance procession begins with each member of the
assembly coming to the place of worship, usually a
church building, and continues in the procession of
the ministers into the assembly. Thus the procession is not just a sign that the liturgy is
beginning, but serves as a transition that
allows the coming together of each person
to be transformed into a communal act of
gathering, welcoming each other and focus-
ing on the presence of the Lord among his
disciples.

At one time all the people assembled in a court-
yard and entered with the ministers; usually now
only those who minister to the community participate in the opening procession. In addition,
sacred objects, such as a cross and the
Lectionary, are carried in procession. Servers
carry candles and incense before the cross
and/or Lectionary to remind us of their importance. The Lectionary and cross remind us that
Christ is present among us. The presence of all the
ministers of the eucharist makes the procession sub-
stantial and dignified.

Gospel procession

The gospel procession allows us to focus on the eternal Word,
Jesus Christ, who will speak in the gospel. The procession, with
its accompanying acclamation, calls us to joy. Servers carry candles and incense before the Lectionary or book of the gospels to
symbolize the festivity and honour given to Christ.

Presentation of gifts

The presentation of bread and wine and the people's gifts for
the poor responds to God's goodness proclaimed in the scripture readings. Having listened to the word of God, we put our
faith in action by collecting money for the work of the church

community. The presentation of bread and wine is a sign of the community's participation in the great act of thanksgiving and offering. It is not only bread and wine that are brought to the altar. The whole community has assembled to offer its service in union with Christ. The link between the community's offering and the bread and wine is strengthened when members of the assembly bring to the altar the bread and wine they supply, if not by baking or providing them, then at least by paying for them. Candles may accompany the gifts to the altar; however, it is not appropriate for the servers to carry candles away from the altar area to the entrance of the church and back for this purpose. Candles may be placed near the gifts, and other ministers may carry candles to accompany the gifts. Practically, it is better that servers do not participate in the procession of gifts, except to assist the priest in receiving them.

Communion procession

The communion procession is the fourth procession of the eucharist and the fourth action of Christ in the liturgy of the eucharist. Rarely is the action of receiving communion viewed as a procession, but it is an important procession. In one way it complements the presentation of gifts. The people of God bring forth bread and wine that the church may give thanks over them. Changed by power of the Spirit, the bread and wine that the church presented are now given back to us as the bread of life and the cup of salvation.

Closing procession

The closing or recessional procession allows the ministers to leave and take up their positions at the entrance of the church. Just as the entrance procession is a sign of the whole community gathering in the sight of God, so the closing procession begins the community's departure in peace to live God's word and be the body of Christ in the world. As in the entrance procession, servers lead the other ministers and carry the candles, cross and incense, if they were used.

General principles for processions

Processions involve walking in public with a group of people who move in a common direction at the same rate of speed. Thus those who participate in a procession must be conscious of others, as well as the direction of movement and their destination. This is especially important for those leading the procession. Please consider the following:

- how fast or slow should you walk?
- where are you going?
- what are you carrying?
- with whom are you walking?

By thinking about these questions and combining them, we can state some basic principles for processions:

- Always be attentive to what you are doing and where you are going.
- Be conscious of your partner and the others whom you are leading: walk beside your partner slowly enough so other ministers do not have to walk too fast to keep up with you.
- When walking around a table or any object, you usually do not separate from your partner, except when there is not enough room for the two of you to walk together.
- Never walk backwards.

Order of ministers in a procession

The church's tradition usually provides for a certain order in the procession. Although these may vary from place to place, here are some basic principles.

- Servers, especially those carrying the incense, candles, and cross, usually lead a procession. Those carrying the incense go first, followed by those carrying the candles. The cross bearer and the lector carrying the Lectionary follow. Other servers who carry nothing in the procession should carry a hymn book and join in the singing.

- The other ministers, such as the lectors and ministers of communion, usually follow the servers.

- The deacon and any other priests come next.

- The priest or person who presides comes last in the procession.

B. Hands and Minds and Voices

What to do with our hands is one of the basic questions for liturgical ministers. If we become self-conscious in public, our hands often betray our nervousness. Learning what to do with them will help everyone relax. For those who are holding something, this will not be a problem. Those who are not holding anything—walking, standing, sitting and bowing—should join both hands at waist or chest level. Walking or standing with hands dangling at the side distracts others and may be interpreted as a lack of training. When only one hand is occupied, the other is placed on the chest.

Once people become familiar with how to serve, there are still many challenges and opportunities for their talents. Learning what happens next, what will be needed next, what the priest and the assembly need next will be the test of a good server. In other words, use your mind and keep it active. Do not daydream. Serving demands full attention. Finally, when something is forgotten, or goes wrong, the true server learns how to cope and adapt. An old sayings is true, "There are no mistakes in liturgy, just great recoveries."

The voice is also important in liturgy. We use it to praise God both in song and word. As members of the assembly, servers should join in the hymns, acclamations and responses of the eucharist. Since they will often be carrying something during the celebration, they will need to learn some responses by heart.

On the other hand, there are times when it is important to refrain from speaking, especially during the times of silent prayer and reflection.

C. Reverences

When two people meet, they usually greet or acknowledge each other. The same happens in the liturgy. We bow or genuflect to acknowledge another's presence, especially Christ's presence in the ministers and in the people of God. In the liturgy there are four types of reverence: the genuflection, the bow, the kiss and the sign of peace.

Genuflections

A genuflection is reserved only for Christ in the eucharist, either reserved in the tabernacle or on the altar in the consecrated bread and wine. A genuflection would be made to the tabernacle by all people on entering and leaving the church, before and after the celebration. On December 25 and March 25 we genuflect during the words "and became man" of the Nicene Creed.

Bows

There are two types of bows: a bow of the head (a nod or simple bow) and a bow of the body (a deep bow). Servers make a simple bow to each other, and to other ministers, including the presider. They make a deep bow to the altar, as does the deacon when asking a blessing from the presider, and as do all the people at the words "and became man" in the Nicene Creed.

Kissing the altar or cross

A kiss is a very ancient sign of honour and respect. The priest and deacon kiss the altar at the beginning and end of the eucharist, and the Lectionary or book of the gospels after reading the gospel; the people may kiss the cross on Good Friday at the celebration of the Lord's Passion.

Sign of peace

Before communion the people recognize the presence of Christ in one another by exchanging a sign of peace, usually a handshake or embrace. At one time it was customary for all Christian people to exchange a kiss, but this is not so common in our country, so we usually shake hands or exchange a hug.

D. Focal Points

Throughout the liturgy various focal points relate to the action that is taking place. Only one point of focus operates at any one time. Something different happens at each place.

1. Ambo (lectern): The ambo is the place from which the word of God is proclaimed. It gives a sense of unity to the liturgy of the word. Servers carrying candles (and incense) accompany the deacon or priest to the ambo for the reading of the gospel.

2. Altar: The altar is the table of the Lord: on it are placed the gifts of the people; at it the great prayer of thanksgiving is solemnly proclaimed, so that the bread and wine may be transformed into the body and blood of the Lord; to it the people of God come to receive the gifts of God, so that they may be transformed into the body of Christ. The altar is used only at the liturgy of the eucharist, and the only things placed on it are the gifts of the people: bread and wine. The only exception is the book of prayers, the sacramentary. The servers set the table by placing the sacramentary, cup and purificator on it. They may help the priest and deacon receive the bread and wine and bring them to the altar. They wash the hands of the priest. After communion they also clear the table.

3. Chair: The chair symbolizes the ministry of presiding exercised by the priest. The introductory rites of the eucharist, the profession of faith, the introductory and concluding prayer of the general intercessions, as well as the concluding rite, take place at the presidential chair. Here a server holds the book of prayers for the priest.

In Summary

1. As a ministry, serving is an exercise of our baptismal priest-hood; it is the giving of ourselves as Jesus did. Liturgy is also repeated action that becomes easier and more familiar over time.

2. One of the basic movements in liturgy is the procession:

   - the gathering of the people and the entrance of the ministers
   - the gospel procession
   - the presentation of the gifts
   - the communion procession
   - the procession of God's people into the world

3. Liturgy and serving involve the whole person: body, mind and spirit. During the liturgy we join in procession, listen, pray and respond in silence and song, make the sign of the cross, sit and stand, give thanks and praise, present bread and wine, break bread and pour out wine, eat and drink.

4. During the liturgy there are three focal points: the chair, the ambo and the altar table.

Discussion Questions

1. What are some of the qualities servers need to carry out their ministry?

2. Identify some of the things that servers carry or hold during the celebration. Why are these important?

3. Discuss the three focal points of the celebration of the eucharist and the role of the servers during each.

CHAPTER 3

The Ministry of Serving

Servers contribute to the ritual and prayer of the celebration by providing atmosphere, movement and preparation. What you do at the Sunday celebration of the eucharist will depend on how many other servers there are, the layout of the church and the setup of the area around the altar, ambo and chair. This chapter suggests some general functions that are part of the ministry of serving.

Step 1: Serving Functions

Several servers may be present at the celebration of the Sunday eucharist. Usually they are named by the function each performs. Servers may fulfill one or more functions during the celebration as follows:

- Cross-bearer: the server who carries the processional cross in the opening and closing procession;

- Book-bearer: the server who holds the sacramentary at the chair for the presider for the opening prayer, the profession of faith (creed) and intercessions, and the prayer after communion; he or she places the sacramentary on the altar for the eucharistic prayer and removes it after communion;

- Acolytes or candle-bearers: the servers who carry the candles in the entrance and recessional processions, and the gospel procession;

- Incense-bearer or thurifer (or censer-bearer): the server who carries the thurible and boat of incense in the processions for incensing the cross, the book of the gospels, the altar, the cross and the assembly.

A. Carrying Candles

Servers carry candles to accompany and highlight the sacred symbols carried in procession, such as the Lectionary or book of the gospels. They may even carry one of these symbols, the cross. Candles (and incense), carried before the cross or Lectionary, are an ancient way of marking these as important objects that represent the presence of Christ among us. While not absolutely necessary, they add an important visual and ritual element to the celebration. They help the assembled people to focus on Christ among them, to remember why they have assembled, and to express in a visible way the faith and love that brought the community together.

Candles are normally used three times during the liturgy: carried before the cross or Lectionary in the entrance procession; before the book of gospels in the gospel procession after the second reading; carried before the cross or Lectionary in the recessional or closing procession.

General principles

- Many different types of candles are used today. Some have large candlesticks that are meant to be placed on the credence table, others are shafts or poles that fit into holders that sit on the floor. In all cases, hold the candles with both hands. They are easier to hold when the left hand is placed level with the waist, and the right hand, level with the chin. On a candlestick, one hand can be placed around the base, the other, half way up the candlestick.
- The candles need to be held high so the people can see them. Partners should hold their candles at the same height.
- The candles need to be held upright so that the wax does not spill. Therefore, servers carrying candles do not bow or genuflect. Simply bow or nod your head when the other ministers genuflect or bow.

- When carrying candles, walk together with your partner, at the same speed. Always face the same direction, and, when turning, turn in towards each other.
- In a procession, walk on each side of the symbol you are accompanying (the cross or Lectionary), or, if there is not enough room, walk ahead of the symbol. When standing on each side of a symbol, such as the Lectionary or gospel book at the ambo or the cross during its veneration on Good Friday, face the symbol.

B. Carrying the Cross

In many churches it is customary to carry the cross in procession to the sanctuary, and to place it in a prominent place for all to see, perhaps near the altar or ambo. However, if a large cross or crucifix is permanently fixed in the sanctuary, the processional cross is placed at the side of the sanctuary.

The cross is normally carried twice in the liturgy: in the entrance procession, and in the recessional or closing procession.

General principles

- The cross is carried with great dignity and reverence. Hold it high so all can see it during the procession. It is easier to hold the cross if you place one hand level with your waist and the other at the height of your chin. Walking at a moderate or slow pace is appropriate.
- When carrying the cross, never genuflect or bow. When the other ministers bow, simply nod or bow your head.
- The cross-bearer does not lead the procession; rather, the two acolytes precede the cross-bearer or accompany the cross, and, when incense is used, the thurifer leads the acolytes.

C. Carrying the Incense

Incense is used as a sign of respect and reverence for God, a symbol of our prayers rising up to God, and a reminder that we are God's holy people. During the eucharist, incense may be carried in the entrance and gospel processions, and used to honour the altar and cross, the book of the gospel, the gifts of bread and wine, the presider and the people and the consecrated elements. The use of incense is optional, and it may be used at any or all of the following times:

- in the entrance procession;
- to incense the altar and cross at the beginning of mass;
- in the procession and proclamation of the gospel;
- to incense the gifts, the altar, the presider and people at the preparation of gifts and altar;
- at the elevation and showing of the eucharistic bread and cup;
- in the recessional procession.

General principles

- One or two servers may assist with the incense. If there is one server, the thurifer carries both thurible and boat and hands the boat to the presider while opening the thurible. If there are two servers, one carries and holds the thurible, the other the boat.
- When carried in procession, a thurible with chains is held at the top of the chain and the thurible is swung backwards and forwards on the side of the body while walking. A thurible without chains is held high with a side-to-side swaying motion.
- In any procession, the server carrying the incense always leads the other servers and ministers.
- There are two types of swings to incense a person or symbol. Double swings are used when one person or symbol is incensed. Single swings are used when a group of people are incensed, or when the altar or Easter candle is incensed by walking around it. Thus the priest is incensed with three double swings; the people are incensed with three single swings.

- When presenting the thurible to the deacon or priest, hold the top of the chain in the right hand, and the middle of the chain in the left. Thus the other person receives the top of the chain in the left hand and the middle of the chain in the right. If the presider is left-handed, you may need to present this in the opposite way.

D. Holding the Sacramentary

A server holds the sacramentary for the presider. This enables the presider to pray with hands extended in the posture of prayer. This gesture symbolizes the unity of the assembly in offering its praise and intercession to God. The arms of the presider embrace the whole assembly, while the palms of the hands are open and raised to heaven to offer up the prayer of the assembly, as well as to receive what God gives us.

The sacramentary is usually held at the chair three times: for the opening prayer, for the profession of faith and intercessions, and for the prayer after communion.

During the preparation of the altar, a server places the sacramentary on the altar for the eucharistic prayer.

General principles

- Hold the sacramentary with both hands at the bottom of the book; the top usually rests on your chest or forehead, depending on your height and that of the presider. Servers should curl the tips of their fingers around the bottom of the book and tuck their elbows in at the side of their body so that they can hold the book securely without too much movement.
- When holding the sacramentary at the chair, the server should not stand directly in front of the presider. Stand slightly to one side so that the people can still see the presider. If the presider is on a raised platform, you should stand on the lower level.

- There should be no movement in the church during times of silent prayer. The server should already be in place when the presider says, "Let us pray"; he or she should not leave until the people have completed the prayer with their "Amen."
- It is helpful to know how to open the book for the presider at the right page; but this is not necessary if the book is held in such a way that the presider can reach the ribbons or tabs to open the book. Make sure that the ribbons of the book are hanging to the side, not at the very bottom of the book.

E. Preparing the Table

Servers prepare the table by placing the corporal, the cup, the purificator and the sacramentary on the altar, assisting with the cruets of wine and water, and washing the hands of the priest. This helps the presider and deacon to receive and quickly prepare and place the bread and cup on the altar in preparation for the eucharistic prayer, when the church gives thanks over the bread and cup.

General principles

- Set the altar much like a dining room table at home. First place a corporal, or on special occasions a table cloth, on the altar. Second, place the sacramentary and an empty chalice or cup on the table. These should not be placed in the centre or middle of the altar since they are not the important things that will be placed on the altar: the priest will place the bread and wine brought by the people in the centre of the altar. Therefore, place the sacramentary and cup close to the edge of the table. Usually the sacramentary goes on the left side and the cup on the right. The chalice is always accompanied by a napkin or cloth (purificator); this, however, should not be draped over the chalice, but placed next to it.
- Usually some of the people will bring the bread and wine directly to the altar. It is normally not necessary for the server to receive these from the people; one server may take the collection to the credence table and bring the pitcher of water to the altar.

- When holding the pitchers of water and wine, remove the tops before presenting them to the deacon or priest. Hold the pitchers with the spouts pointing towards the people, so that, when the deacon or priest takes them, the spout is pointing in the right direction for pouring wine or water into the cup.
- The priest's washing of hands will depend on the size of the pitcher and bowl. If these are large and heavy, one server holds the pitcher and pours the water, the other, with a towel draped over the arm, holds the basin. If they are light enough, one server holds both pitcher and basin and pours the water; the other unfolds and holds the towel.
- When leaving the altar, the servers bow to the priest or deacon by nodding their head.

F. Clearing the Table

If the priest and communion ministers return all the plates and cups to the credence or side table, then, during the communion rite, the servers clear the altar by returning the sacramentary, corporal, purificator and any remaining vessels to the side table. Here the vessels will be cleaned, preferably after the celebration. When the altar has been cleared, all return to their places for a time of silent prayer.

If the priest cleans the sacred vessels at the altar, then, after the communion rite is completed, the servers will need to bring the pitcher or cruet of water to the priest. The server brings the water to the side table and returns to the altar to get the sacred vessels and bring them to the side table. Once the altar has been cleared, all return to their places for a time of silent prayer.

Step 2 - The Order of Things

A. Eucharistic celebration with two servers

The Acolytes
1. Entrance procession

- carry the candles in the entrance procession, leading the person carrying the Lectionary or book of the gospels;

- bow to the altar as they arrive, or with the other ministers after all have reached the front of the altar;
- place the candles in their stands near the altar or on the credence table; and take their place near the credence table or the presidential chair (but not flanking the presider).

2. Opening prayer

- one of the acolytes holds the sacramentary for the opening prayer.

3. Gospel procession

- after the second reading, the two acolytes take the candles from their holders and lead the deacon or presider to the ambo (lectern) for the reading of the gospel;
- stand one on each side of the ambo, facing each other;
- after the gospel, return the candles and go to their places.

4. Creed and intercessions

- one of the acolytes holds the sacramentary for the creed and the intercessions.

5. Preparation of the altar

- as the collection begins, the two acolytes go to the credence table. One acolyte places the sacramentary on the altar and the other places the corporal, one chalice and purificator (cloth) on the altar.

6. Procession of gifts

- after the collection they may assist the presider in receiving the collection and gifts of bread and wine from the people;
- one places the collection in a suitable place; the other holds the cruets of wine and water.

7. Preparation of the gifts

- after the gifts are prepared and placed on the altar, return the cruets of wine and water to the credence table and get the bowl and towel for the washing of hands;
- return to the altar and stand ready to wash the presider's hands;

- remove any unnecessary items from the altar: hymn books, missalettes, top of the flagon of wine, etc.

8. Eucharistic prayer

- participate with the people in the eucharistic prayer and sing the acclamations at the appropriate times.

9. Communion rite

- after the sign of peace, bring the remaining chalices, purificators (cloths) and communion plates (ciborium) from the credence table to the altar;
- during communion, remove the sacramentary and all other items from the altar;
- one of the acolytes holds the sacramentary for the prayer after communion.

10. Recessional procession

- after the dismissal, servers take their candles and stand ready to leave the sanctuary;
- bow to the altar with the other ministers and carry the candles in the procession to the main entrance of the church.

B. Eucharistic Celebration with Three Servers

The acolytes

Same as above.

The Cross-bearer/Book-bearer

1. Entrance procession

- the cross-bearer carries the processional cross in the entrance procession, accompanied by, or following, the acolytes;
- bows to the altar and places the processional cross in the stand;
- takes a place in the sanctuary near the presider.

2. Introductory rites

- holds the sacramentary for the opening rite, if necessary, and the opening prayer.

3. Liturgy of the word

- holds the sacramentary for the creed and the general intercessions.

4. Preparation of the altar and gifts

- during the collection, the book-bearer places the sacramentary on the altar while the acolytes place the corporal, chalice and purificator on the altar.

5. Liturgy of the eucharist

- during the communion procession, the book-bearer removes the sacramentary from the altar;
- holds the sacramentary for the prayer after communion.

6. Concluding rite

- holds the sacramentary for the final blessing, if the solemn form is used.

7. Recessional procession

- after the dismissal, the cross-bearer takes the processional cross and stands ready to leave the sanctuary with the acolytes;
- bows to the altar with the other ministers and follows the acolytes to the main entrance of the church.

C. Eucharistic celebration with incense

The Acolytes

Same as above.

The Cross-bearer/Book-bearer

Same as above.

The Bearer of Incense: the Thurifer

Another server may assist the thurifer and carry the boat, the container for the grains of incense.

1. Entrance procession

- the thurifer carries the thurible and boat and leads the procession to the altar;
- bows to the altar upon arrival, or bows with the other ministers after all have reached the altar;
- waits for the presider at the altar for the placing of incense;
- after the incense has been placed, the thurifer gives the thurible to the presider and goes to the side of the altar and waits for the presider to complete the incensing of the altar;
- after the incensing of the altar, the thurifer receives the thurible and returns it and the boat to their places.

2. Gospel procession

- immediately after the second reading, the thurifer gets the thurible and boat and goes to the presider at the chair for the placing of incense;
- leads the acolytes and deacon (or presider) to the ambo (lectern) for the proclamation of the gospel;
- stands behind the ambo while the acolytes take their places on each side of the deacon or presider;
- the thurifer hands the thurible to the deacon or presider;
- after the gospel the thurifer returns the thurible and boat to their place.

3. Preparation of altar and gifts

- during the collection the thurifer checks the charcoal and lights a new one if necessary;
- during the procession of gifts, the thurifer gets the thurible and boat, and stands ready near the altar;

- opens the thurible for the placing of incense for the incensing of the gifts, the altar and the people;
- incenses the presider and the assembly.

4. Recessional procession

- after the dismissal the thurifer takes the thurible and boat, and stands at the side of the altar with the other servers;
- bows to the altar with the other ministers and leads the procession to the main entrance of the church.

In Summary

1. The act of serving centres around carrying the cross, candles or incense; holding the book of prayers (sacramentary) and the water and wine pitchers; and preparing and clearing the table of the Lord.

2. Normally two or three servers share the ministry of serving at the celebration of the eucharist. Some aspects of serving require two servers, such as carrying the candles; others require only one server.

Discussion Questions

1. What is the purpose of carrying the cross, candles and incense in the liturgy?

2. How are servers chosen and prepared for ministry in your parish?

3. Who is responsible for training, coordinating and scheduling the servers in your parish?

4. For the servers to carry out their ministry, what things are needed at the chair, at the ambo and at the altar-table?

5. How can servers pray at the celebration and still carry out their responsibilities?

The Mystery We Are Called To Be

Paragraph 58 of the *General Instruction of the Roman Missal* echoes the *Constitution on the Sacred Liturgy* when it reminds us that everyone in the eucharistic assembly has the right and duty "to contribute their participation in ways differing according to the diversity of their order and liturgical function." This means that everyone contributes to the celebration, not only by their liturgical ministry, but also by their personal and individual gifts. This is a vivid reminder that together we are the body of Christ, and individually we are members of that body. Each one of us is important in God's plan of salvation, in the worship of the church and in the life of our parish community.

Lucien Deiss states that all render fitting service to community: the priest who delivers a wonderful homily, the elderly lady who prays softly, the sick person who offers their illness to God, the organist who moves us to shiver, the little boy who sings and fidgets throughout the celebration, and the person who composed the music for the celebration. All are part of the mystery of what the church is and who we are as the assembly that gathers to worship. I hope that you will not only be a good minister to the community, but also be conscious of the great mystery that we celebrate—the mystery we are called to be.

For many centuries that mystery and wonder of serving God was sung and prayed by the choir and assembly of people in Psalm 42. It served as the entrance hymn to the celebration of the eucharist. Later it was crystallized in the "Prayers at the foot of the altar," which every server recited with the priest. Very appropriately, the refrain stated, "I will go to the altar of God, the God who gives me joy." I hope that this book will help you serve God and give you the joy that flows from God through us as we seek to follow Jesus.

A. The Church Building

Aisle(s): the passage way(s) between the rows of pews or chairs in the main body of the church which allow the people to enter and leave the worship areas.

Baptistry: the area where baptisms are celebrated. It may also refer to the baptismal font itself or to the location of the font—at the entrance of the church, in a separate room or area, or close to the altar.

Confessional room: the room or place where the sacrament of reconciliation is celebrated.

Narthex: the area or hallway between the outside doors of the church and the interior doors into the worship area. May be called the vestibule, atrium or porch.

Nave: the main body of the church where the people of God gather for worship. Derived from the Latin word for ship, which is often a symbol for the church. Also called the worship area.

Sacristy: the room(s) used by the ministers to prepare for the celebration of the liturgy and the place where the vestments, vessels and other things used in the liturgy are stored.

Sanctuary: the area of the nave around the altar, ambo and chair.

B. Furniture

Altar: The principal and central focus and object of the eucharist, the table of the Lord to which God's people are called to give praise and thanks to God, on which they place the gifts of bread and wine, and at which they are fed and nourished at the banquet of the heavenly kingdom.

Ambo: the place, stand or desk from which the word of God is proclaimed. Also called the lectern.

Chair: the presidential chair for the presider at liturgy; symbolizes the teaching authority of Christ entrusted to the church.

Chairs or pews are also provided for the people of God (see pews).

Credence table: the small table at the side of sanctuary on which are placed the things needed for the celebration. May also be called the side or serving table.

Lectern: see *ambo*, above.

Pews: the rows of long benches for the seating of the assembly.

Presidential chair: see *chair*.

Tabernacle: the locked container in which the eucharistic bread is reserved after the celebration of the eucharist. Normally placed in a separate chapel to reserve the blessed sacrament for communion of the dying and the sick, and for adoration. From the Latin word for "tent," and from the tent used by the Hebrews for the ark of the covenant. May also be called as "the place of reservation."

C. Vessels, Cloths and Objects

Acolyte candles: the two candlesticks carried in procession by the servers or acolytes to accompany the processional cross, Lectionary or other sacred object.

Boat: the container, round or oval in shape, for the grains of incense which are placed on the charcoals in the thurible or censer. Normally contains a spoon for placing the incense on the coals.

Book stand: the cushion or holder for the sacramentary used on the altar during the eucharistic prayer and communion rite.

Censer: see *thurible*.

Chalice: the cup (usually of gold) used at the celebration of the eucharist in which wine and a drop of water are placed.

Ciborium: the plate or container that holds the bread for the celebration of the eucharist.

Corporal: the large square, white linen cloth placed in the centre of the altar on which are placed the cup and plate for the celebration of the eucharist.

Cruets: the pitchers for the wine and water.

Funeral pall: the large white cloth placed over a casket during the funeral mass as a reminder of the baptismal robe.

Incense: the grains of sweet-smelling gums and resins placed on burning charcoal to produce fragrant smoke, a sign of the prayers of the people rising to God, of our reverence for God and the symbols of Christ's presence in the liturgy, especially in the assembled people.

Lavabo dish: the basin or bowl used in the washing of hands at the eucharist.

Lavabo towel: the cloth used to dry the hands of the presider at the washing of hands at the eucharist.

Lectionary: the large book containing the scripture readings proclaimed at the celebration of the eucharist during the liturgy of the word.

Pall: a square, white covering for the chalice or a large, rectangular, white covering for a casket (see funeral pall).

Paschal candle: the large candle blessed at the Easter Vigil as a sign of the risen Christ. Stands near the altar or ambo for the fifty days of the Easter season and near the baptismal font for the other seasons of the year.

Paten: the flat, dish-like plate for the eucharistic bread.

Processional cross: the cross attached to a long pole for use in processions.

Purificator: the long and narrow cloth (napkin) used to wipe the chalice.

Pyx: a small container used to carry the consecrated bread from the eucharist to the sick at home or in the hospital.

Ritual book: a book containing the prayers and texts needed for the celebration of the sacraments, other than the eucharist. For example, baptism, confirmation, marriage, funeral and blessings.

Sacramentary: the book containing the prayers and text for the celebration of the eucharist (sometimes incorrectly called the missal).

Sacrarium: a special sink, usually in the sacristy, where holy water or water used to wash the cloths of the eucharist goes directly into the ground.

Sanctuary lamp: the lighted candle or lamp that burns continuously near the tabernacle or place of reservation as a sign that the blessed sacrament is reserved.

Thurible: the metal or pottery container (censer) in which incense is placed. Those with chains may be carried and swung at celebrations; others may be pot-shaped containers placed on a table.

D. Vestments

Alb: floor-length white garment with sleeves worn by those who minister at the altar. Symbolizes Christ and the royal dignity received in baptism.

Chasuble: large, sleeveless outer vestment worn by a presbyter or bishop at the celebration of the eucharist. May be purple, white or gold, green or red in colour, depending on the liturgical season or celebration. Purple is worn during Advent and Lent; white or gold during Christmas and Easter and for feasts of saints who are not martyrs; green during Ordinary Time; red is worn on Passion Sunday, Good Friday, Pentecost, and the celebration of martyrs. The Latin word for chasuble means "little house," referring to the large size of the vestment, which covers the priest.

Cincture: the cloth or cord belt tied around the waist and alb.

Cope: large cape worn at celebrations outside the eucharist, such as baptisms and marriages, morning or evening prayer, and benediction. It may be the same colour as the chasuble.

Crosier: shepherd's staff carried by the bishop as a sign of his office. It is also called the pastoral staff.

Dalmatic: large, outer vestment of a deacon. It is the same colour as the chasuble, but differs from it by its square cut, long sleeves and two vertical bars on the front and back.

Mitre: the pointed hat worn by a bishop or abbott as a sign of his office.

Stole: long, scarf-like piece of coloured cloth worn by the ordained. May be worn alone over the alb for celebrations and concelebrating at the eucharist. Worn by the deacon over the right shoulder, hanging down the back and front like a sash. A bishop or presbyter wears it around the neck with both ends hanging down the front. Same colour as the chasuble.

E. *Terminology*

Benediction: the word means the act of blessing or praising God. A devotional ceremony of prayer and praise for Christ present in the consecrated bread of the eucharist. Its name comes from the concluding rite of the ceremony when the people are blessed by the priest or deacon who makes the sign of the cross with the eucharistic bread placed in a special vessel called the monstrance.

Communion under both kinds: act of receiving the body and blood of Christ by eating the consecrated bread and drinking the consecrated blood of Jesus.

Concelebration: act of celebrating the eucharist by a number of priests gathered around the bishop as a sign of the unity of the ministerial service of Christ to the church.

Consecration: transformation of the bread and wine into the body and blood of Christ during the eucharistic prayer.

Doxology: Greek word meaning "word of praise." May refer to any prayer of praise, but especially refers to the concluding section of the eucharistic prayer: "Through him, with him, in him."

Elevation: lifting up of the consecrated elements at different points in the eucharistic prayer: after the institution narrative and at the doxology.

Eucharist: central act of worship of the Catholic Church, especially on Sunday, the Lord's Day. Composed of two major parts, the liturgy of the word and the liturgy of the eucharist. After listening to the word of God, the people of God, led by an ordained minister, take bread and wine, give thanks to God for the action of Christ, break the bread and pour the wine, and eat the body and blood of Christ.

Eucharistic prayer: central prayer of thanksgiving in the celebration of the eucharist, when, in the context of praising God for the saving action of Christ, the church asks God to change the bread and wine into the body and blood of Christ and to transform the people present into the one body of Christ. Second action of the eucharist.

Exposition: word meaning "showing"; at benediction, the placing of the host (consecrated bread) before the people for adoration.

Fraction rite: act of breaking the bread into small pieces from the one large bread for the communion of all present. Third action of the eucharist.

Genuflection: act of reverencing God by which the right knee is bent to briefly touch the floor.

Homily: proclamation of the word of God given at the celebration of the eucharist or other sacramental rites; based on the readings.

Intinction: method of receiving communion under both kinds by dipping the consecrated bread into the consecrated wine and placing it on the tongue of the communicant. This method is not recommended for use in Canada.

Litany: prayer consisting of a series of invocations, titles, petitions and acclamations alternated between a cantor and the people. Examples: Litany of Saints, Litany of the Blessed Virgin Mary, etc.

Octave: celebration of a major feast which lasts for eight days. Example: octave of Christmas and Easter.

Preparation of the gifts: first action of the liturgy of the eucharist in which the altar and gifts or bread and wine are prepared, brought and placed on the altar.

Proclamation: solemn reading of the word of God, the eucharistic prayer, or prayer of blessing in a sacramental rite.

Purification: act of cleaning the sacred vessels used in the communion of the eucharist.

Reservation: keeping the consecrated bread in a tabernacle for communion to the dying (viaticum), the sick and for adoration.

BIBLIOGRAPHY

Recommended Readings

Documents

Ceremonial of Bishops. Congregation for Divine Worship, translated by International Commission on English in the Liturgy, Collegeville, MN: The Liturgical Press, 1989. Also in *The Liturgy Documents*.

Constitution on the Sacred Liturgy, Vatican II, 1963 in *The Liturgy Documents: A Parish Resource*. Chicago: Liturgy Training Publications, 1991.

General Instruction of the Roman Missal. 4th edition, 1975, Congregation for Divine Worship, in *New Introductions to the Sacramentary and Lectionary*. Ottawa, Canada: Canadian Conference of Catholic Bishops, 1983, and in *The Liturgy Documents: A Parish Resource*. Chicago: Liturgy Training Publications, 1991.

Books

Archdiocese of Kingston. *Ministering at the Altar of the Lord*. Office of Liturgy, 390 Palace Rd, Kingston, ON Canada K7L 4T3.

Bernardin, Joseph Cardinal. *The Ministry of Service: An Introduction to Ministry*. Collegeville: The Liturgical Press, 1985.

Deiss, Lucien, CSSp. *Persons in Liturgical Celebrations*. Chicago: World Library Publications, Inc., 1978.

Dunn, Greig S. *The Server*. Toronto: The Anglican Book Centre, 1978.

Fauque, Michel. *Petit guide des fonctions liturgiques*. Paris: Téqui, 1983.

Kwatera, Michael, OSB. *The Ministry of Servers.* Collegeville: The Liturgical Press, 1982.

Lanz, Kerry J. and Post, W. Ellwood. *The Complete Server.* Wilton, CT: Morehouse-Barlow Company, Inc., 1978.

Lebon, Jean. *How to Understand the Liturgy.* Lymington, Great Britain: SCM Press Ltd, 1991.

Nevins, Albert J. *Called to Serve: A Guidebook for Altar Servers.* Huntington, Indiana: Our Sunday Visitor, Inc., 1981.

Video

Kwatera, Michael, OSB. *Training the Mass Server.* Collegeville: The Liturgical Press, 1989.

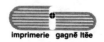

imprimerie gagné ltée